Jere Truer is a poet, essayist, storyteller, and musician who made his living as a psychotherapist in private practice in Minneapolis. He currently teaches at Adler Graduate School. He was married for many years to Tamara Chaney Truer, who passed away in 2002. It was the onset of her breast cancer that first inspired a joint endeavor of her journal and his poetry about the path of healing. Alas, her death ended that project and Mr. Truer resumed the project on his own with this book. He re-married to Monica Schurtz and lives in Arizona.

Dedicated to my daughter, Kate Whooley, and to the memory of Tamara Chaney Truer.

Jere Truer

THE ART OF DYING

AUSTIN MACAULEY PUBLISHERS™

LONDON • CAMBRIDGE • NEW YORK • SHARJAH

Ordering Information:
Quantity sales: special discounts are available on quantity purchases by corporations, associations, and others. For details, contact the publisher at the address below.

Publisher's Cataloging-in-Publication data
Truer, Jere
The Art of Dying

ISBN 9781641822497 (Paperback)
ISBN 9781641822480 (Hardback)
ISBN 9781641822503 (E-Book)

The main category of the book — Poetry / General

www.austinmacauley.com/us

First Published (2018)
Austin Macauley Publishers LLC
40 Wall Street, 28th Floor
New York, NY 10005
USA

mail-usa@austinmacauley.com
+1(646)5125767

Published Works

The Whole Catastrophe was published in "The Wind Blows, the Ice Breaks", Nodin Press, 2010. *A Walk at Dusk* was published in "The Cancer Poetry Project", Fairview Press, 2001. *When You Sneeze* was published in "Bedford Poets", Red Dragonfly Press, 2007.

Part I

A Ghost in the Life

If there is an explosion out in space,
Does anyone hear, or can anything be heard?
And if your life implodes and there is profound loss,
But no one asks after you, can you be heard?

Tamara died fifteen years ago after four years
Of battling… No, let's stop that right here.
There is no battle, because that implies weaponry
On both sides, as well as an army and a fighting chance.
When a long-distance missile strikes a home
In the midst of quietude, for no good reason,
There is no battle, no war, no strategy.
And the screaming, the wailing, and moaning,
As well as the bleeding amid the rubble
In the aftermath, is not a response but a result.

So, Tamara died as a result of cancer.
There was nothing we could do about it in the end.
Or the beginning either, though we thought we could.

Or I thought I could. I was small as a child.
An only child in a home of secrets and shame.
My father drank and became meaner as he went.
My mother looked to me for succor, for rescue.
For answers to the unanswerable.
I just did as I was told: I came up with answers.
And I came up with rage to meet the demons.

It was a spiritual and intellectual rage
That I met life with. And that was a battle.
Although one I could never win
And one I could never admit to losing.
Nevertheless, I did some good in the world,
As I gave comfort and safety where needed.

But I could not save my wife.

I have been standing in hip-deep rubble
For all my life. But because I stand,
Because I do not wail and moan,
Because I stand and I stand and I stand,
No one comes for me,
No one comforts me.
I do not seem to need it, they all say.

When I go back to the scenes of my life,
I pass among them as a ghost—invisible,
Unheard, unnoticed, nor can I remain.

How does one grieve except
To crawl across the ruined floor
And work up to standing?
As for me, I now walk with a limp.

The Beginning

She was not my type.
In fact, a bit scary to have as a girlfriend.
A colleague or neighbor, yes. But smart
And tall and mother to a young girl.
And angry over a recent divorce.
I was looking for fresh and young,
Someone I could impress.

A lot of men orbited her,
A few men drove to places in the city
With which she was still unfamiliar.
We had drinks and others drove her home.
I was never one to take another man's woman,
Much less a friend's. I knew her for months
When David asked if I had called her yet.

So I called her. She asked what took me.
I am not the kind of guy who gets the girl.
And when Michael, David, Paul, and, and…
There seemed to be so many
Holding her train. Good guys all.
And who the hell was I
But a scruffy, bad poet with pocket change?

She broke my heart. Not in any usual
Way, but because she was sure, sweet,
And generous, and I was scared.
She broke my heart because I could see
I could break hers.

If there is a moment that makes a man,
It's when he sees the harm he can do

And turns away from it, to give in,
And allow himself to be loved.
We moved in together a year later.
And then we were wed. Kate haltingly called
Me Daddy, and I did not refuse.
The usual happened: renting houses, then
Buying, grad school, and orthodontia for Kate,

Cello lessons, piano lessons, family vacations,
And deaths in the family. My father,
Her mother. We had two dogs,
A gerbil for a while, till it tried to eat its
Way out of the plastic cage and died.
There were two storms of the century.
One in summer, flooding the basement,

And the other dumping four feet of snow.
Friends married, friends divorced,
Friends miscarried. There were fights;
She was afraid of anger till I provoked
Her into slamming an upstairs door.
It locked and there was no key.
I rescued her with a ladder to the window.

It was a marriage; it was a life.
There was laughter and mirth, tears
And fumbling confusions with sex and money,
Uncertainty with careers.
But I knew she believed in me, I in her,
As we made it through nearly two decades
While the world seemed new on its skates.

When Kate was in high school,
We took in an exchange student from Germany.
Princess Diana was killed, and John John,

Then Mother Theresa died.
Just before Christmas, one morning,
I reached into her nightie to make my move.
Ouch, she cried out, and we both sat up.

Her Breasts

She was always ambivalent about her breasts.
Quite beautiful and round, envied by women,
Coveted by men, but reserved at last for Kate
And for me. But for years, her Uncle Jack
Cracked, *"What ya got under that sweater?*
A coupla wrestling pigs?" Her mother's older
And bullying brother. No one stood up
To him nor for her. So her sweaters grew
As camouflage and shelter. She was ashamed.
And no one in the rural backwoods of Indiana
Would defend or rescue her. She went north.
We all found her beautiful.

I found her beautiful, as well as her breasts.
And on that morning, as I reached beneath
Her gown, she gasped as I touched a hard spot
Just below her nipple. Do you know how fear
Piles a bushel full of snow upon your belly?
How the earth stops turning on its axis?
We tried to push all alarm aside and carry on.
But there was no lovemaking that day.
Just swirling questions and frantic attempts
At a benign answer. She would go to no doctor,
For the Indiana doctors had finished the damage
Begun by Uncle Jack.

Psychics and mediums were consulted:
It was merely a plugged duct, and energy,
With light, would unclog it. I believed in God,

The holy corporate structure of angels and devas,
The lords and ladies of the Light, I did.
And it was Christmas time as well, the season
Of uncanny miracles. But the lump was weedy,
Pernicious, and strong: it grew and kept growing.
And she would not go to the god-damned doctor,
Till one day in spring, I said I could not watch
Her die in front of me. If she would not go in,
Then I wanted a divorce.

The Diagnosis

When we wed, it was for life—
It was not for death. I would not marry
Death. Too much time there already.
So she chose life, chose fear,
Chose facing the wounds of childhood.

Her breast lump was biopsied
When the doctor could aspirate no fluid.
I waited in one of those horrible hospital rooms
They over-try to make comforting and 'healing,'
While you act like you are in church:

Faithful, hopeful, patient but secretly
Losing your mind. And the mindless TV
Cheerfully broadcast news of Linda
McCartney, who just died earlier that day,
Having succumbed to breast cancer.

If you are outside on a calm day
With no wind and a feather falls from a tree,
You watch it make broad arcs in the air
As it makes its inexorable descending diagnosis,
Yes/no/maybe/yes—invasive ductal adenocarcinoma—

As it lands leaden in your numb hand,
In your now-numb life where everything else
Strikes you dumb, except the words 'I love you'.
So you repeat them over and over and over
As you drive her to Matt's Bar.

It is where you sat with her and many others
Before the courtship, as the attraction grew.
It seems to be the only place to go that makes
Any sense somehow. You stand with her on Cedar
Avenue, as you did then, holding on and not letting go.

The Oncology Waiting Room

It seems to try so hard not to be what it is.
I was hospitalized for eye surgery in 1956.
When hallways were narrow grey corridors,
The floors were scuffed, checkered linoleum.
That is how it should be when this frightened.
The light was dim, yellowish, receding.
I watched my father's grey car coat slowly
Disappear down the hallway as he left.
Throughout my childhood, I would look
Down the wrong end of a telescope and feel
Lonely. No comfort except for the nuns.
Now, there are comforting pictures everywhere,
An aquarium with large tropical fish,
Although they are just as helpless and trapped.
There is a painting of Christ healing the sick.
He wept for the suffering it costs us each
Just to be alive. And he had his own scarred
Feet, which must be why he insisted on
Washing ours with his tears.
Does he hear us as we sit amid unread magazines,
Styrofoam coffee cups half-filled with oily
Cold coffee. Listen to the whispered refrain:
Help me, help me, help me, help me.

Crazing the Vessel

Our human bodies are encased invisibly
In the secret of not-knowing, not-supposed-to-
Know, that allows us innocence of the gods
And of the ways of the gods. It's only when
We die that we break out of that cocoon,
Knowing everything once more.

Many of us, however, are not so lucky
To travel this earth without at least a crack
In our spirit shell. Tamara had hers smashed
At an early age, and she bore the unbearable
Gift of knowingness. She knew that I knew too,
And we tried to keep that a secret.

What did we know? We knew, somehow, she
Would not grow old, that Kate would be
Orphaned, and so I needed to be there for her.
And we knew all kinds of things about Druids,
Past lives, mystery schools, and that this joke
About cancer was only a mistake.

What didn't we know? We didn't know this
Project of a journey (Don't you love it? Journey?
The implication of arriving somewhere safe?)
Through cancer was really a trial of facing death.
I did not know I would have all my spiritual
Assumptions rendered meaningless.
So do I still want to be a psychic knower,
To have my vessel shell split to splinters

So that I would appear crazed when glued back
Together? Is there really a together once rent
Apart? Why is it when they ask who died,
The god's honest answer is "I did".

How a Man Loves a Woman

I think it was God who chased me,
But I could be wrong, in my dream
Down flights upon flights of stairs
In the hospital stairwell.
If it was God, where was Grace
I prayed to overleap the railings.
Where was mercy?

Perhaps it was in awakening
In the wee hours and arising,
To wash a load of clothes,
Pay the doctor's bills,
And watch for the break of day.
I will welcome it in.
This is how I love my wife.

Banyan Trees

There are trees in Hawaii where the boughs
Grow out only so far and then plunge down
Back into the earth to become more roots
For the tree. I grew up too, then I grew
Back down. People think I am sad
With all this muddy water circulating
Through the filaments of my heart.
But the tree does not choose this life,
Nor do I, other than to live it.

All this circling causes a time out of mind.
Past or present—it does not matter.
I walk through the rooms of my house.
In the living room, Tamara is still alive,
Watching sci-fi TV shows with Kate.
I am still in the kitchen, alone in the house,
Washing the dishes of the past.
In still another living room, my current
Wife in my current life makes a present future.

Things thought crucial disappear.
Tamara started a journal of how she survived
Cancer, I wrote a bunch of responding poems.
A week ago, I plunged into helpless darkness
When I could not find even a scrap of them.
Did I throw them away? Perhaps.
I have lost, or thrown away, my mind at times.
Even thought about burning down the house,
But I was drunk, it was late and very cold outside.

Fifteen years out, so far, I still smell the smoke.
A different fire cleansed me, burned off the dross.
The dry underbrush, the windswept trash,
The faded ink on crinkled paper with messages
From an invalid future, from an invalid past;
They all went to ash. A friend read my palm
Years before saying a death in my 50s would
Set me free. I guess it's true. And it is true
What they say: with freedom comes responsibility.

Keeping on Walking

When someone decides to get married,
It is preceded by a sense of despair.
It is the fatigue and discouragement
Freighting the dreams gone heavy
By carrying them alone.

Two weary travelers meet
At the hot and dusty crossroad
In the afternoon. Each is tired,
And four roads head in each direction.
They decide to make do right there.

When one gets restless and bored
And begins to remember early dreams,
The spouse is there to remind them
How foolish it is to live in the past;
How happy were they really?

Or there are those who, once refreshed,
Keep walking. Many go on alone,
And that is as it should be.
But I was lucky to find a companion
Who could see the sacred mountains.

She began the journey with me.
Then she went on ahead.
She cheated by shape-shifting
While I have to trudge along behind.
Will she recognize me when I arrive?

The Whole Catastrophe

It has been nine years in this house,
Thirteen in this neighborhood.
The waitress at the local café
Asks me if I'll have the usual.
I never thought I'd be predictable.
And yet I've come to covet the reliable,
The time worn, the perennial ways
That men and women have on this earth.

I spend today raking leaves,
Caulking the cracks, keeping winter
And all its rodential companions outside.
I'll take this seasonal death of crumbling
Rock, fallen leaves, and soft ground.
I'll call it life, I'll call it home.
On this I rely for the time we have
Together—this whole catastrophe of love.

A Walk at Dusk

In mid-August in Minnesota,
Dusk falls in grey-colored particles
On tree boughs, on roof tops,
Across yards and fields,
Bearing the earth downward
Into sweet melancholy.

The retiring sun's wan smile
Bids us release, permission
To let it all go, every last bit
Of what was unrequited this day,
This year, this life.

So, it is when you and I
Walk each evening near the creek
Past the dozing houses near home.
Old grudges slough off me,
Like clay dust, and are licked up
By the paths of the hungry earth
Since death came to live with us.

Immigrant Waltz

The hospital wanted $12,000
We did not have.
It took me two hours to write
One check after circling the desk
That day, and many other days.
Hand quivering and gut gnarled,
I emptied myself of the future.

When we looked down the hall of futures
To see something appear, it did not.
No doors opened, the light dimmed.
An old janitor mopped the floor,
Oblivious to our distress.
Perhaps the world was through with us,
But there were still the two of us.

Our forebears crossed a wide, endless
Ocean on faith and hope alone,
Having left one impoverished shore
For an uncertain, unwelcoming one.
They wanted not wealth, but justice—
To say one's prayers openly;
To say this is me, that is mine.

And so we chose to do the immigrant waltz
On old planks thrown on the bare ground
Of the little plot we called home.
Yes, our hearts were breaking then,
But the moon and the breeze and the night

Were free. And I loved her even more.
I said this is me and you are mine.

Empty Hands

I miss looking down at your hands
The way they used to lie across mine.
Your fingernails, your knuckle creases,
That scar from when you were a girl,
Absent-mindedly ironing clothes.

Now, my hands hover
With no one to hold.
They hover in empty space
The way the heart hovers
Vacant after the burial.

I bade you slip inside my heart
When you left, and as you have gone
Across the wide waters of eternity.
Will you wait for me, wherever you are,
As I await you here?

Finding a Name

There is a name for breathing
Underwater while terrified,
While amazed, while in bliss.
The world requires fresh names
When the immigrant
Arrives as someone else.
Or when the apron of the woman
Darkens upon marriage,
Then each subsequent child.

There are so many things
I have hidden, or forgotten—
Is there a difference?
One by one, she called them out.
And called me by my true name,
Which I had forgotten,
Or hidden.
It was a new language,
And I called all those things

Tamara.

Loathing the Sound of My Name

Times there were I loathed the sound
Of my name. As when she called it
From across the house or the upstairs
Bath. I would find her collapsed
On the floor, drenched in sweat,
Vomitus around her mouth.
As when she would howl it
With a wild animal yawp,
Or whimper it into my soaked shirt,
Her fingers clutching the fabric
With the same ferocity the chemo
Writhed through her guts.

I was absolutely useless,
Save to grab a bucket, a cool rag,
Or hold her hairless head in my hands
While the night had us stopped dead
On its tracks—it would not yield day.
Nothing—nothing—I had ever done
Even mattered in that naked moment.
We were all alone at the bottom
Of the world, a pathetic Adam and Eve
After the expulsion, calling God's name
In vain to only a silent response.
Perhaps he, too, hates the sound of his name.

Spirits

How many mystics does it take to change
A light bulb? None. You just love it as it is
Until its own light shines from within.
Tamara did not have cancer; she was not
Dying. This was all an illusion perpetrated
By a fear-based medical establishment.
Ask me if I believe that. Oftentimes I do.

August 2nd was an ominous date.
The second shoe drop, and last August 2
Before she died, we finally surrendered
And our home became a hospice.
The first shoe drop came after she was
Cured, and then more tests were run.
A year-and-a-half at the most.

All an illusion, all an illusion.
We heard of a spiritual healer in Saint Paul
Whose miracles were covered by the local
News, by the science reporter, a skeptic.
Yet he was convinced, and we were convinced,
And we went on TV to tell the world.
We were the John and Yoko of illusion

All we were saying is give cash a chance;
Thousands of our few dollars fed the illusion.
We bought special stained-glass windows,
Imbued with spiritual and angelic light
And made by our multiply-gifted healer.

And the more we bought, the more we could
Hang in our windows for the angels to see.

I overheard the healer whisper to Tamara
That God hated her but Jesus loved her.
Also, that she would never see Kate again,
But Kate would see a comforting image,
Thinking it was her. Thus was the healer fired.
And then it was August 2nd, the 2nd.
I saw a sign selling spirits and I bought a lot.

Kenosis

September 11 is forty days after
August 2, when she was diagnosed
Metastatic. Cells had been hiding,
Colluding, conspiring, and then
Big explosions. It was in 2001.
We had our anticipatory apocalypse.
Then the world caught up to us.

I heard a woman say she had lived past
The point of living being good for her.
I heard a man say we are lost when
The inner world does not match the outer.
Abraham Heschel prayed to a grieving God
To come down out of exile—
If only for a moment.

It is called *kenosis* when God empties
Himself of divinity and power,
So that His feet get bruised
By our stones, His hands
By our refusal.

What is it called when
We are emptied out,
When we stand in the rubble-strewn void
Where even angels wring their hands?

As Usual

Five months after the radical mastectomy—
During which she endured chemotherapy,
Which made her wretch and heave dry,
Then radiation, which burned her skin raw,
Followed by doses of Prednisone that blew her
Up like a kids' magician's tied balloon---
She cooked dinner for the first time.

I had come home late, crabby from traffic.
Kate came home hungry. But not for the
Stir-fry she had labored to cook.
Any ceremony she wanted or expected
Was sorely lacking. Any sense of the normal
Ways of the household long-abandoned;
We were now in an occupied territory.

She forgave us as she always forgave us.
And would probably forgive me now,
Though I do not feel I deserve it.
Although, were we looking for a return
To normal, we found it in this homely
Scene with us as our tawdry selves. I would
Give anything for things to be like that.
To be as usual.

Part II

The Gatherer of Souls

The face can be seen in the glint
Of light on my wedding ring.
A face I first saw looking at me
Behind my grandfather's coffin,
When I was three and saw heaven
For the first time.

He watched me suffer fools,
Entertained by bad ideas for too long,
All while following bad advice.

I have been driven up winding, crumbling
Mountainous roads where down
Below was nothing but ash.
I arrived sore-footed in small gambling towns,
My wrecked car left far behind.

I have heard my name called
In abandoned hotel hallways
Where the voice always comes from
The next room, or one level up, or
One level down. When I say
I am here, there is no response.

The game is rigged, the prize hidden,
And the only way to leave the table
Is to not care about what happened,
Not to care about what happens
If you do not care about what happened.

For whatever will happen or not happen
Will go on whether you care or not.

I watched him slowly pack my wife's life
And cart it away, before coming back for her.
I sit here by the heels of God,
Writing about my greatest teacher,
But it is so goddamned hard,
So goddamned hard to praise him.

Hermitage Lines

I

A snowstorm accompanied me
Through the woods along iced and curved
Narrow roads. I have over-rehearsed
My stories of how I came to be here,
Where I am, but they have become my
Burden; I can carry them no longer.
This is the end of my life
As I have known it. I limped in here
Broken and I may not walk out.
All we need know is that a storm,
A great storm, howls outside and everything unessential
remains in drifted snow.

II

I could write that words fail me,
But it is I who fail words, fail history,
Fail God. My dreams anticipated
How I would stand up to speak
But could not read the text.
Words written in wind-whipped
Snow. Ice-laden branches crack, snap.
I married you without giving up
My solitude. And so I keep it.

III

The clock of the world has been cleaned.

The floor, however, reveals the broken glass
And blood. The doctors gave you a year.
The storm rages elsewhere for now.
An otter serpents around the snowdrifts,
Through the tamaracks and oaks,
Into the thicket beyond.

IV

For five nights, a young woman has lain
Her petal-scented head upon my dreams.
Now, at the beginning of the sixth night,
She rebukes me, saying,
"I came to you once—
"I will not come again."
My sleep becomes the blizzard.
There is no direction towards waking
That will bring me back to the house.

V

All day I stare into the woods.
Only the trees and the sky move.
After dozing—animal tracks all around!
There are many things which happen
When no one watches.
How you died silently in front of me,
How you keep dying and remain,
With your terrified eyes,
Back in there somewhere,
Amid the fractals of ruin.

VI

Looking up from my book,
The night comes,
Just as it told me it would.
I look out into the reciprocal

**Darkness until I become no
One, nothing.**

Whatsoever

Now that I've clung to life
On an iceberg in the steaming seas,
Having cheated death of any theft,
I find myself washed up back away
From the sinking hospital beds, away
From plastic tubing, pill bottles,
Midnight liquor sweats, catheters, IV tubes,
Saline bags, syringes, O2 bags,
Washed up in an utterly new land,
Confessing ignorance daily,
Reading more poetry, fewer newspapers,
Listening to silence, receiving flowers,
Falling in love with two dogs running
Down the street, barking past boys
Playing catch on the street, between cars,
On a summer evening as the whole world—
There is only one woman—
Turns within me, without me, while suffering
Joy blows through the colossal void within
Atoms without any explanation, without
Any explanation whatsoever.

Naked

After the radical mastectomy
Where her left breast was excised,
There were puckers of flesh, fluids draining,
And tubes coming out of her chest.
The surgeon said there were clean margins,
Meaning she got absolutely all of the diseased
Flesh. But there were lymph nodes still
Where cancer cells scattered, like terrorists,
Into the confounding, mysterious chemistry.

I checked the incision several times a day,
Giving her a description of the healing she could
Not and would not see. Getting ready for bed,
One night, I watched as she crossed the room
Naked. I wept inside for her ravaged body,
And how she once rejoiced in the hunger I had
For her breasts, their cool pliability beneath
Her clothes. She asked if I still wanted her.
I was older; I insisted on her.

Years of Pilgrimage

1

Birds at the feeder. Liszt on the stereo,
'*Annees de Pelirinage*,' solo piano.
One can feel the knapsack worn
On mountain trails, heavier
With each renunciation.

A blue jay clambers about the thick bark
On the ash tree, sinking its toes deep
Into the crevices to keep perpendicular;
In the snow below, cat prints.

2

Every night this week, I dream
A young woman rests her sweet head
On my shoulder. She tells me I had her
Once, but no more; I wake up weeping.

I can forgive you, I say to the woman,
To everyone I meet who talks to me.
This game has been rigged. We, losing,
Must only be gentle with one another.

3

Afternoon can find me listening.
Everyone says the same thing, wanting
Pardon. Then, shadows grow

While the sun slips by, unnoticed.

Evening approaches, windows light up.
A woman stands before a kitchen sink.
A man rises to close the curtain, a child
Practices the piano—will never stop
Practicing.

Stones at My Feet

To you whom I have loved, and love still,
Now among the dead, but ever more alive,
I say *God be with you*, which is goodbye,
Or farewell. But we have no word for a
Complete ending—not even *dead* does it.
Not since going abroad in that country.
I began an unfinished conversation
Between us, and I suppose no ending.

And so, God be with you as you dwell
In the wind around me, in the caves
Of my heart. I have spoken no words
Which work to bring you closer,
Nor which send you out of my thoughts.
Ah, Irish girl, I do find you down
By rivers and streams, in wooded glades,
In the damp earth sogging my feet.

As I have gone on living and dying,
The world only entertains me now,
Held between the edges
Of your eternity.

The Worst That Happens

The worst that can happen often does.

A man goes down in a plane crash
Who could have stopped a war.

A woman's daughter screams how loathsome
She is and leaps from her mother's moving car.

There is no use in worrying.
Plan on it. Fix the roof.

But when it rains, walk outside.

It is not a matter of deserving or not
Deserving. Something else happens.

The one who, along the bombed-out road,
Nudges the wildflower from the asphalt crack
Called me to get back up.

The best thing happened.

My exploded heart sprouted
Up from its seeds.

Three Crows

In a dream, I return to one of those places
From which I have been away too long.
When was I last here? Don't know.

It is as familiar as it is unfamiliar.
Who knew I would wear these clothes
Or look like this? Whose hands are these?

A silken shroud burning to ash floats
Above me. Somewhere upriver,
A funeral pyre; three crows fly past.

Many times I was so unkind to her.

Long Playing

Back in the days of long playing,
She had only fifteen of those vinyl LPs,
Those of Judy Collins, Joan Baez, Janis Ian,
Among other gentle folk whose sweet sounds
Burbled on her portable stereo.

                                She
Kept them in a wooden peach crate, lugged
Them from one studio apartment to the next.
Missing sleeves, torn at the edges, finger-
Smeared, scratched; all of these the marks
Of the love she had.

                        Once at the Cathedral
Del'Orte, in Venice, Tintoretto's church,
I saw the Madonna in marble by the altar.
After vespers, the aging parishioners cupped
Mary's face, stroking her and kissing her.
She was worn, smooth, and oily, featureless,
Valuable perhaps only to eternity now.

I was the Protestant and the protestant:
I kept my records clean, crisp, scratch-less,
Wiped free of any dust or DNA, not a tear
Or any sign of wear, alphabetized even.
And I gathered hundreds of them.

                                She
Is gone now, out of both our lives, leaving

Behind in our attic a remnant of her sloppy
Love. A love which now clutters memory,
Disorders my routine on a day intended
To clean up my own mess. Wherever she
May be, may she know that, though I loved
Differently, I have learned some messy
Extravagances in these disordered years.

Forgetfulness

You won't forget me, will you?
She asked this of me just days before.
I swore I would remember everything,
Always. And then the years pass.
Many of the things we packed for the journey
And loaded up on the horses got jostled
On the rough roads, got rained on,
Got soggy and rotten. They fell away,
And there is no going back for retrieval.

Perhaps it is the job of the living to gather
For usefulness, while the dead have in mind
A disappearance, a forgetting.
The souls have to move on, after all.
Too much memory can hold them back.
But I keep what is necessary: remembering
Her touch, her voice, what she achieved,
How she laughed, and those mornings I awoke
Empty and scared and how she held me.

She's Leaving Home

Upon the wooded ridge above Terre Haute,
Near the Wabash River, an almost fairytale
House—dark-stained wood, stone foundation,
Leaded glass windows—sits deep in the woods
At the end of a long drive, slowly sinking.

She grew up there, all alone.
There was a sister, but they fought.
There were parents, and they fought.
Often which child was the favorite.
There was an ultimate tie: they both lost.

Only the ghosts of mobsters who hid out
During the Depression and a Civil War soldier
Near his sunken grave to talk to, she lived quietly
With her books, her daydreams, and a few records.
One of which was *Sergeant Pepper*.

After she died, I put her twenty-odd albums
In the attic. Having had only one or two friends,
No teen in the 60s showed her how to care
For them; they were unplayable, all scratched.
Except for *Sergeant Pepper*, barely played

But for '*She's Leaving Home*.'
How many tens of thousands of times
Did she listen to that track, weeping, pleading
For the courage to leave? To be finally noticed
As a human being, not a decoration?

A very pretty, tall, auburn-haired Irish lass
In her cable-knit sweaters and corduroy.
Ophelia of the Wabash Valley amid the sprites
And faeries, moving through the mists.
Beautiful, yes, but not a decoration nor a toy.

What to Do with a Widowed Man

What to do with a heart that opened
Beneath a warm, nourishing sun, and overcame
Its wary seclusion? She was not the first to teach
Love to me, but she was the most patient
When the waters of grief let loose from all
Those lonely years, knowing aloneness herself.

The hermit had come down from his retreat,
Had opened his collar and removed his cloak.
And when I found myself alone again afterwards,
I could no longer navigate the cold mountain
Paths leading to the craggy perches of solitude
And had to go crazy, down in the villages.

As women approached me, I did not lurch
But longed with all that was within me
To have them open their dresses to me.
There certainly is a lust which is lascivious.
And just as certainly one, perhaps greater,
Commensurate with death's embrace.

Within eighteen months, I remarried,
While enduring the snickering of women
And the relief of married men who saw in me
Their worst fears realized, then assuaged.
And, though, the denouement should now come,
I still missed the one who was gone.

Please be kind to the widowed man.
Let him pour out his tears and rage.
Drink with him and carry him home
Without branding him a hopeless drunkard.
As the waters of grief flow around you too,
Do not flee, nor swim, but weep. Just weep.

Medical History Form

After profound loss, you experience your own
Death, and every little wound or infection
Insults your once intimation of immortality,
And your medical history form drives it home.

Contusions, fractures, surgeries, falls,
Accidents, and car wrecks; the brief account
Of each, including dates and outcomes—
The elaborate cascade of catastrophes.

You watch the physician's furtive eye
Scan this chronicle of abuse and neglect.
Were there a body protection service,
Mine would be placed in foster care.

Neither exonerated nor castigated,
I am sent home with an assignment
To be gentle. And the doc puts a hand
On my shoulder to reassure me each time:

No, I do not have cancer.

The Cry

What woke me in the early morning
Was a cry from someone bestial or ghostly.
Not from within me, but from behind—
Somewhere dark and deep.
I had dreamt of an angel who came here
But could not get back home,
Who fell into lonely matter.

A liquid sun melted behind the dunes
As the one no longer holy stood
Watching. You know the sound he makes.
And so do wolves and the trees who beckon
With uplifted branches. It says:
I am here while you are over there.
And the distance is uncrossable.

Akasha of Regret

A silent surreal film by Luis Bunuel shows
A man pulling wagon loads upon wagon loads
Of every single thing possible to put there.
The metaphor was the weight of conscience
Upon the modern soul all the way back
To the Original Sin. I vowed not to amass regret.

I regret I did not keep that vow, and I regret
Much, very much. Two months after the death,
I came home late to find Kate wrapped up
In her mother's clothes and scarves.
She had gathered what she could find
And piled it all upon our bed, weeping.

I had not shared that bed for two months
Was now paralyzed by my powerlessness
To pull Kate from the wreckage and detritus
Of loss. And so, I pulled her out and away.
It was something ragged, raw, and snarling,
And yet not enraged—just hopeless.

Kate was an only child who gave her mother
A reason to live, a reason to leave Indiana
And to begin healing. Refugees they were,
And clung to each other at first, and then last.
I was envious, admiring, heart-broken,
And protective of it. I could have done better.

How could I struggle with the weight

Of my own grief and carry hers, too?
Whether or not I was drunk, I stumbled
Down the endless road with no destination
Other than forward, just forward, and much,
Much fell off and down, never to be found.

Watching Wild Strawberries

While she was dying in her hospital bed
In the middle of our living room,
With her medicine bottles and emesis basin,
And stacks of pads to soak up urine,
With the portable toilet nearby,
I watched old movies. When I could.
Meaning: when I could concentrate.

For a week, the movie classics channel played
Bergman's '*Wild Strawberries.*'
I wept the rest of each day upon viewing.
Perhaps it was because my grandfather
Otto, dead for fifty years, was Swedish.
And I can still hear, if I listen closely,
His soft Swedish voice call my name.

Or perhaps I see my future in old Isak Borg,
Who goes to bed each night an aloof man
Who has confusing dreams. Have I held
So much back? Do the people I love
Know how much I love them? Or will they
Watch me from behind, with my rumpled clothes
And mussed hair, pitying and wondering?

The girl at the end, in a white dress,
Walking through shimmering grass
By the lake where wild strawberries grow,
She guides Professor Borg through reverie,
Through innocence, back to simple kindness,

Despite his regret. And she looks just like
The photo of my wife at that age.

Black Smoke

Sometime during the years of her cancer,
I dreamed a recurring dream
Where I drove a rural two-lane road
To God knows where.

Up ahead, a plume of black smoke
Gave its inky generosity to the sky,
Billowing and ebbing in dispersion,
Seeming so close, yet far away.

There was no way around it,
As it lay dead ahead on my path.
Should I have gone another way?
Who or what caused this catastrophe?

Those questions were useless then,
As well as now. There are no excuses
For whether we are dead or alive at times,
And there is no turning back.

Many years later, there is still a smudge
On the horizon behind me,
Seeming so far away, yet so close—
Space and time ever more irrelevant.

Not Turning Away

A story I heard was back in college
Was that a film-maker shot reel upon reel
Of film footage documenting cadavers
Lying, like hunks of blue clay, on the grey
Morgue slabs. The nauseated, terrified
Film-maker's hands shook, causing the film
To jerk and lurch on the screen.
Word is, he wanted to truly see death
And overcome what was left of his denial.

I thought of that story many times
As I sat beside her bed, where she continuously
Died—continuously, relentlessly, and gradually.
Of course, that is how we all go, not in the end
But right now, and for all of our lives. And death
Comes not at the end, but after the end;
The end of career, or marriage, of money,
Of hope. And you sit there at the bottom
Of yourself and dare anyone to talk about God.

Just Some Guy

For half an hour I was just some guy,
Scribbling in a book near an indoor fountain
In a downtown office building under construction.
I smelled nothing that smelled like life,
Nor did I hear anything moving or alive
That trembled; no one knew my name.

While walking the windowless sheetrock
Corridors of this empty, echoing space,
It occurred to me that were I in a movie,
This is where I would be murdered.
The killer would be famous, but I
Would go uncredited, anonymous.

But that would be alright.
The logic of my perverse fantasy
Was that I would be expendable—needed
By no one, having no karmic debt to pay.
I could have changed my name to Steve,
Just some guy scribbling in a book.

When You Sneeze

I must bless you
Even if
No current science
Supports demons
Rushing into
The vacancy
Before inspiration,
After expiration.
Perhaps your soul left
Your body after
All, if only
For a glimpse
Of the sacred
Mountains.
Yet I remain,
Yet I bless you.

An Occasional Poem

Because I was caught again
Amid the dry, scattered leaves, pieces of
Board, among the weeds, by the worn wooden
Gate the wind insisted on teasing...

Because the train rails disappear
Past the grain silos, and the road parallel
Disappearing too; and the rows of corn,
But they all go on forever...

Because the grasses of the cemeteries
Finish the job of dying by growing tufts
Of sod around crosses, over the gravestones,
And all names, all dates, all words...

Because the stars ultimately frighten me
By their distance, their constancy, how
One comes into being, how another is gone,
How much of what we see is no longer there...

Because of snow melting star-like,
Coral-like, in the crusts at the lake's edge,
Freed by the warmth of a spring day
And the onion grass dancing...

Because of melancholy, which gathers
All these little worlds which decay yet remain
Faithfully at the periphery. And sadness
Mixed with sweetness bids us bless...

Arguing with the Dead

The dead cheat in any number of ways.
First, it is in their act of dying: they just leave
You standing wherever it is you are.
And then some part of you is forever stuck
In the vacuum of their vanishing act.

Also, when they are dying, their demise
Trumps anything else that goes on.
If it happens quickly, it is not so bad.
But a long illness means weeks, months,
Sometimes years of getting the short straw.

They want to go to Pompeii before the end,
And then perhaps Machu Picchu.
You really cannot afford that and need
A break. But you have the rest of your life
To dig out of the debt; and they are dying.

You can get angry, argue, even shout
At them as they lie there so pathetically,
Balefully looking at you with no strength
Left. And there you stand without a shred
Of decency left, and they will not fight back.

Afterwards, in the Big Afterward, loved ones
Canonize their sainthood, create shrines,
Deify them even. But only a sentimental grief
Cleanses them of their humanity, their flaws.
To truly grieve is to admit the truth:

They are imperfect, as flawed as the rest of us.
They do not always fight fair and took advantage
Of you at times, or sabotaged you unconsciously.
They often ran late and forgot things, and orphaned
Their children, deprived everyone of their presence.

And you are left with only memories.

Leaves

I am raking leaves—maple, ash, birch,
Magnolia, oak—some from my yard,
Most from the neighborhood around.

I am sinking in a bottomless pile
While new ones, blown from the street,
Riot the already-unruly crowd of them.

I am thinking of you, whoever, wherever
You are, as you read this poem.
These leaves are the result of deciduous

Nature—the perennial deciding done—
The perennial *killing by sword* we commit
Every day of our lives, choosing.

So, I stand here among the dead, the fallen,
Wondering what to do next. Is there an end
To what has piled up? Choosing—

To leave something behind in my gathering,
Discarding many things—having them blow away.
I can only keep just so many things alive;

The trees remain. And so do we, you and I,
Windblown and tattered, perhaps, but
Standing. And letting go of what leaves.

Looking at My Hands

Even now…funny, that phrase,
As though the soul's important work
Has an expiration date, a statute of
Limitations… But even now,
For it is always now with the soul's work,
Grief stops by for a late-night chat.

The house no longer empty,
But everyone is asleep. Even beyond
Here, all the windows are dark.
He said no one else would put him up
For the night, and he saw I was awake.
He asks for a drink, but I cut him off.

I look down at my hands in my dark lap,
So often useless in times like these,
Barely able to hold a pen or play a note.
Palmists say one hand tells your original
Plan for your life, and the other the way
It really is; what a difference!

During the first years when he came
To visit, he stayed longer, moved in.
We had an arrangement where one night
I would just load up the car, drive away
Slowly, headlights off. Looking out
The window—a tree full of crows.

Closure

How often do we hear this word? Closure.
It is as though the door we opened into the room
Of suffering can finally be closed.
It was never believed to be easy to do,
But with enough effort one could crawl up
The tilted, slippery floor and close that door.
And if it was not done in sufficient time,
Then turn your back and walk away;
Live in the present moment, let the past
Pass, what happened yesterday is only a memory.
Do not believe it!

Only those with secrets to keep
Need to close the books on the accounts
And silence the historians. What are you
Afraid of? That your past life will show
And tell on you? Well, you are correct.
It does show, and a stream of ghosts follow
Behind each of us. That is why we have wars.
That is why there is so much poverty
And sickness. But ghosts do not want this:
All they need is recognition, not revenge.
So turn around!

So many spectral lights surround me.
If you count up all my poems, you know
How many there are. Yes, many are sad,
Some angry, some forlorn, but they are ghosts
Who only want my love, to be heard out.

Mary Shelley wrote a novel about that:
She just needed her father's blessing,
And her creature just needed such
In order to be done with the world.
So many rooms in my house; so much
Have I loved, it sometimes breaks me.
But I am also loved in return.
This poem, my gratitude.

The Art of Dying

She died in the early fall,
Before the leaves fell, but as they turned
To display their true colors, they flamed
Out in the deciduousness of their life.
Like the soul showing itself, finally.
It occurs to you that you will die,
Perhaps in the same way, if lucky.
That is the first lesson in the art of dying.

But you knew, you thought, already
That you and everyone around you will die.
And you knew that she was dying.
The two of you went to the Pentagon,
Met with the Joint Chiefs of Staff
In the war on death—their blue uniforms
And white lab coats. Their meticulous strategy
Sequestering the enemy in the art of dying.

You always thought of yourself
As the reasonable one, who could sit down
And pull a cooling truth out of the flames.
Things will always get better, you said,
Until that one cold, dark morning
When she sat shaking on the toilet,
Blood pouring out of her. *"I'm really going to die,"*
She said, all hope lost in the art of dying.

The imminently dying master the art
With a four-year degree, but for those of you

like me, it involves decades of post-doc study.
On your own. Up until the moment of death,
There is always hope of an abrupt turn
That leaves you careening into the ditch.
But the head-on collision was averted.
But we can't avoid wreckage in the art of dying.

After the circus of funereal proceedings
Leaves town, after the beautiful tear-stained
Flowers dry up and are swept away, after
Neighbors stop bringing food, your house
Grows cold and turning up the furnaces is futile.
Your life is over. Your cold bed is your coffin.
There may be life after death, or reincarnation,
But all you know is nothing in the art of dying.

When the cyclone takes the town, the town rebuilds.
Where wooden structures stood, now stand brick.
Either that or they move into a yurts or wigwams
Meant to be abandoned as climate changes.
At first, you rebuilt with stone and timber a fortress
Against the chaos. But frost and wind, rain and thaw
Still hold the day. The bigger you build your bulwark,
The bigger the collapse in the art of dying.

All things must pass away, and hold, though, you will,
The pull towards loss remains stronger than attachment.
The one who died has gone trippingly on their way
Into the mist, into eternity, into heaven, or just gone.
There is no say to be had. The rest of your life
Falls away as you live the rest of your life. It does not
Matter. What held you up really held you down.
And complete freedom glimmers in the art of dying

Part III

Long Train Coming

I still remember it was October 7th,
At ten past four, and it was a Monday—
Cloudy with spits of early snow till then.
And when her face opened in astonishment
Upon her death, the sun came out, swear to God.

Every day after that, for many weeks,
I would watch the clock for ten past four,
Whether a Monday or not. Then, it faded
To only Mondays, then only late afternoons.
There is a Doppler Effect in grief.

With the oncoming locomotive of loss,
The roar is excruciating, deafening,
As you lie back on the railbed for death's
Horrible undercarriage to chug above you.
Then the high keening wail of the echo.

It echoes for a very long time, ever fading
But never gone. Sometimes, you wonder
Whether your ears will ever stop ringing.
When you finally stand up, you come to
Realize it is you who are now a long train,

Stretched out for decades along the track.
Wherever you go, whomever you befriend,
A part of you is here, another part there.
And a good portion is somewhere else.
You are claimed by a tribe in the Other World.